3/9/2000

grades 3 - up

# My
# Little House
# Crafts Book

# THE LITTLE HOUSE BOOKS
## By Laura Ingalls Wilder

## OTHER LITTLE HOUSE CRAFTS BOOKS

# My Little House Crafts Book

18 Projects from
Laura Ingalls Wilder's Little House Stories

BY *Carolyn Strom Collins* & *Christina Wyss Eriksson*

ILLUSTRATED BY *Mary Collier*

HarperTrophy®
A Division of HarperCollinsPublishers

*For our sons, Drew and Aaron*
—C.C. AND C.E.

*To Elizabeth and Emily, who always understand.*
—M.C.

# Contents

# Introduction

The stories told by Laura Ingalls Wilder in her nine Little House books have been read and loved by millions of readers since their initial publication in the 1930s. In these books, Laura gave her readers a portrait of an American pioneer family—her family—as they traveled in covered wagons across the frontier, homesteaded in new territories, farmed the rugged prairie land, and settled frontier towns.

Because the Ingallses often lived miles away from any stores, and because they had little money, they made most of the things they needed by hand from simple and readily available materials—for example, corn husks, brown paper, and buttons. Some of those handmade things made chores a little easier on the frontier, like the willow-bough broom Pa made for Ma when they lived in their little house on the prairie. Some they made just for fun, like Laura's corncob doll or Carrie's button string. And some, like Alice's straw air-castle or Ma's embroidered breadcloths, brought beauty and decoration into a life that was filled with hard work and seemingly endless chores.

Now, in *My Little House Crafts Book*, you will learn how to make some of the same items that Laura wrote about in her books. In doing so, you will be sharing a part of Laura's frontier days as well as making lovely items for your family and friends, and for yourself. On the pages that follow are instructions for eighteen crafts that Laura described in her Little House books. The materials for each of these projects are available at most crafts or sewing supply stores, and the step-by-step instructions are easy to follow. Just remember to read the instructions for each craft through from beginning to end, so you know what to expect!

Knowing how Laura and other pioneers lived, worked, and "made do" with what they could fashion for themselves from the simplest of materials allows us to appreciate their creativity and innovation. Today, when we make some of those things for ourselves, even just as decorations, we pay a small tribute to the generations that sacrificed many of the personal comforts and conveniences of settled society to face the challenges of the frontier.

*Laura had only a corncob wrapped in a handkerchief, but it was a good doll.*
*It was named Susan.*
LITTLE HOUSE IN THE BIG WOODS

# Laura's Corncob Doll

Laura's doll was made from a dried-out corncob. Little girls in log cabins and claim shanties all over the prairie had corncob dolls like Laura's, because they were easy to make and because corncobs were always plentiful. They could also be easily replaced if they were lost or got too dirty. Ma may even have used one of the hundreds of corncobs left in the barnyard when the horses had finished eating the corn kernels off of the cobs to make Laura's doll.

Ma would have drawn a face on Laura's doll with a black pencil, or she might have dipped her "little red pen that had a mother-of-pearl handle shaped like a feather" in some ink made from a mixture of water and soot from the fireplace. The handkerchief for Laura's doll might have been one of Pa's old bandannas. These red or blue cloth squares printed in fancy designs were popular as handkerchiefs at that time. The handkerchief might also have been one of Ma's pretty white cotton or linen handkerchiefs, or a fabric scrap she had saved. You might like to have several kinds of handkerchiefs for your own corncob doll, some for everyday and some for "dress-up."

To make a corncob doll, you will need:

*Large ear of corn, with husks and silk still on*
*Sharp knife*
*Table knife or spoon*
*Two 12" pieces of string (optional)*
*Colored pens*
*12" square handkerchief, or a 12" square piece of calico*
*Safety pin*

**1**. Remove husks and silk from the ear of corn, and set them aside.

**2**. Ask an adult to cut the raw kernels off the corncob with the sharp knife. You can scrape off the remaining bits of kernel with a dull table knife or a spoon.

**3**. Scrub the corncob in soap and water.

**4**. Let the corncob dry out thoroughly. You can put it on a cooling rack so that air can get to all sides. You can also set it outside to dry in the sun, but make sure you turn it from time to time. Drying the corncob may take a day or two. You will know it is dry when it feels very light, dry, and rough. Now you are ready to make your doll.

**5**. To make the simplest doll, draw eyes, a nose, and a mouth right on the top part of the corncob.

**6**. Spread the handkerchief or cloth square flat on a surface. Place the corncob on top of the fabric, and wrap the cloth around it. If necessary, fold the handkerchief so it will fit snugly around the corncob. Sew, pin, or tie the cloth closed as you wish.

**7**. For a more realistic doll, you can add cornsilk for hair and draw the face on a piece of dried cornhusk. First, dry the cornsilk and cornhusk at the same time that you dry the corncob.

**8**. Soak the cornhusk in warm water for about 10 minutes, dry it with a towel, and set it aside.

**9**. Lay a handful of the dry cornsilk across the top of the corncob, centering it so that it hangs down equally on two sides (like pigtails). This will be the hair.

**10**. Fold the piece of cornhusk over the top of the corncob to hold the cornsilk in place. With a strip of the husk, peeled from one edge, or with a piece of string, tie the husk in place about 2" down from the top of the corncob. This will be the face.

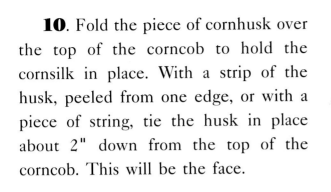

**11**. Using the colored pens, draw a face for your doll on the cornhusk.

**12**. Wrap the handkerchief around your doll as described in step 6.

# Charlotte's Straw Hat

When Pa harvested his crop of oats in late summer, he "cut the heads from several bundles of the oats, and brought the clean, bright, yellow straws to Ma." Ma then made hats for everyone in the family by braiding the oat straws together, and sewing the braid around and around. When she finished the hat, she shaped and dried it in the hot summer sun.

Even though Laura was only five years old, she carefully watched Ma and learned how to make a little hat for her rag doll, Charlotte.

To make a small straw hat for one of your dolls, you will need:

*A bundle of oat straws or a bundle of natural raffia (Raffia is available in*
*craft stores and may be easier to locate than oat straws; you can also use it*
*to make Pa and Laura's Hay Sticks on pages 44–45.)*
*Pan of water*
*White thread*
*Needle*
*Scissors*
*Narrow ribbon*
*Thimble (optional)*
*Dried flowers (optional)*

**1**. Soak the oat straws in water for several hours or overnight, until they are soft and flexible. You do not need to soak the raffia strips.

**2**. Select three straws or raffia strips and knot the ends together firmly.

**3**. Braid the straws. As you near the end of each straw, add another one to it by overlapping the ends about an inch and continuing to braid.

**4**. Keep braiding until you have 2 to 3 yards of braid. Tie a knot in the end. Soak the finished straw braid in the water as you work on it. You do not have to soak the raffia braid.

**5**. Thread the needle. Bring the two ends of the thread together, and tie a knot to hold them. You now have a double thread to sew with.

**6**. Coil the braid into a flat round disk like a mat, and sew the edges together as you continue to coil. This will be the top of the hat.

**7**. When the top of the hat is large enough for your doll (about 1" to 2" across), coil the braid tightly and at a right angle to the top of the hat so that the braid will draw in to make the crown, or the sides, of the hat. Sew as you coil.

**8**. When the crown is deep enough (about ½" to 1" deep), coil the braid more loosely, as you did for the top, at a right angle to the crown. Sew the braid so that it lies flat. This is the hat brim.

**9**. When the brim is as wide as you want, cut the end of the braid diagonally so that the long side of the point is on the inner edge of the brim. Stitch the end firmly to the brim so that it will not unravel.

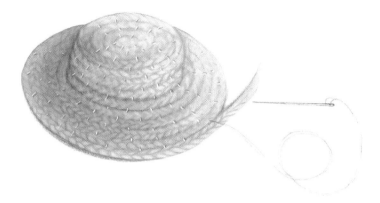

**10**. Soak the straw or raffia hat in warm water for a few minutes.

**11**. Remove the hat from the water, and shape it with your fingers so that the top is smooth, the crown is rounded, and the brim is flat. Let the hat air-dry completely for a day or two. If necessary, set some weighted jars or cans around the brim to keep it flat while it's drying.

**12**. Decorate the hat with the ribbon. You can also add a few dried flowers, if you like.

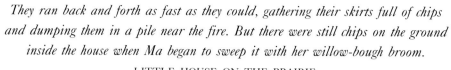

# Ma's Willow-Bough Broom

Before Pa put down the puncheon floor in the little house on the prairie, there was only a dirt floor. Still, Ma wanted the house to be as neat and clean as possible. So Pa gathered slender branches of willow trees, tied them together around a stout stick for a handle, and gave the broom to Ma. It was not as efficient as the broom that Pa bought Ma for their next little house by the banks of Plum Creek, but it worked just fine. Ma kept it in one corner of the little house, so it was handy anytime she needed it.

To make a willow-bough broom, you will need:

*3-foot-long stick, about 1" to 1½" in diameter*
*Several handfuls of willow branches, each about*
      *2 feet long*
*2 yards of heavy twine*
*Heavy-duty scissors*

**1**. Gather the thicker ends of the willow branches evenly around the lower 6" of the long stick.

**2**. Weave the twine in and around the ends of the branches and around the long stick to hold them together.

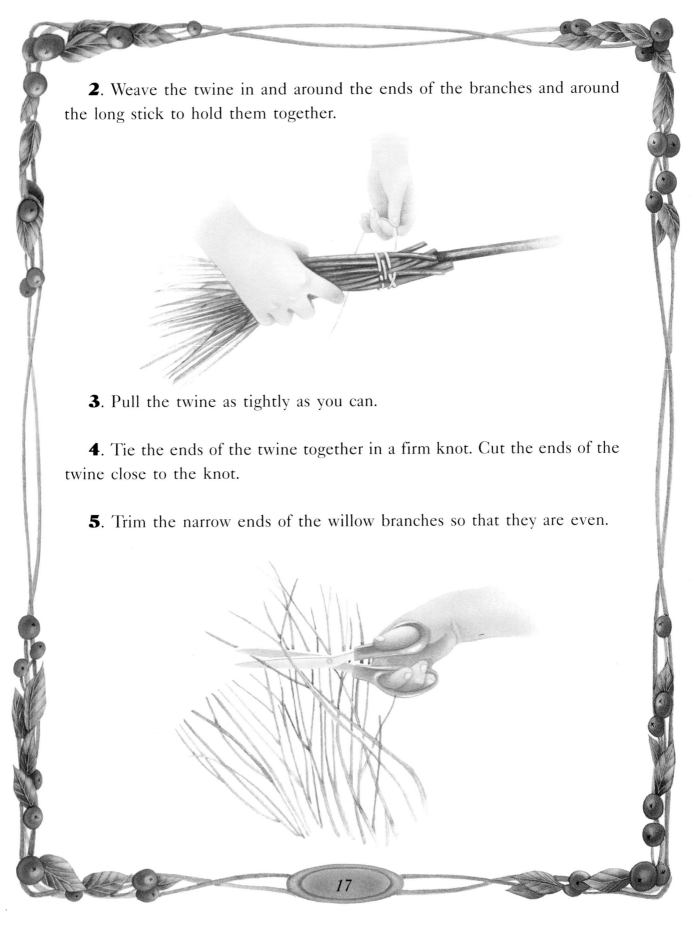

**3**. Pull the twine as tightly as you can.

**4**. Tie the ends of the twine together in a firm knot. Cut the ends of the twine close to the knot.

**5**. Trim the narrow ends of the willow branches so that they are even.

*In the daytime everyone was busy. Pa hurried with his plowing, and Mary and Laura*
*helped Ma plant the early garden seeds.*
LITTLE HOUSE ON THE PRAIRIE

# Ma's Prairie Garden

One spring morning, after a long winter in their snug cabin on the prairie, it was time to plant a garden so that the Ingalls family could have fresh vegetables to eat. So when Pa went into Independence in the earliest days of spring, he bought seeds for turnips, carrots, onions, cabbages, peas, beans, and even watermelons. He said to Ma, "I tell you, Caroline, when we begin getting crops off this rich land of ours, we'll be living like kings!"

Before the garden could be planted, Pa had to plow up the thick grassy prairie sod. The strips of sod turned upside down as they came off the plow. The earth was now ready for seeds, and Ma and Mary and Laura planted their seeds in these strips of rich dirt and matted grass roots. Ma planted tiny cabbage seedlings that she had started in a shallow wooden box filled with soil, and she planted shoots from one of the sweet potatoes that Mr. Edwards had brought across the icy creek for Christmas.

The big garden had to be watered often. Ma and Pa used water from the well Pa had dug the year before, one bucketful at a time. The peas and beans and onions had just begun to sprout when the Ingallses had to leave their little house on the prairie. Soldiers were coming to move all the settlers out of Indian Territory, and Pa decided to leave before the soldiers got there. They ate the potatoes before they left, but the rest of the vegetables were not yet ready to harvest.

To plant a small prairie garden, you will need:

*Vegetable seeds or starter plants (among the easiest to grow are radishes, lettuce,*
*spinach, carrots, peas, and beans)*

*Garden tools—a spade, a hoe, a rake, and a trowel*
*Fertilizer (optional)*
*Flat wooden or plastic sticks (optional)*
*Waterproof pen (optional)*

**1**. Select a sunny spot for your garden.

**2**. Decide how big your garden will be. Mark the edges with a string, some sticks, or even a few rocks so that you will know just where to dig. You can make your garden square or rectangular. Perhaps you would like to plant your garden in the shape of a wagon wheel to remind you of Mary and Laura's trips in the covered wagon! Leave narrow strips of grass in place, or lay bricks or boards down for the "spokes," and plant your vegetables in the spaces between.

 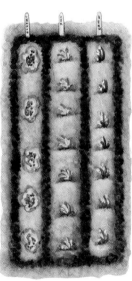

**3**. With a spade, turn over the soil in the space you want to plant. You will want the soil to be nice and loose so that the tender roots of the new plants can grow easily. Mix some fertilizer in with the soil if you wish, following the directions on the package about the best time of year to plant the seeds. Find out from your local garden store which fertilizers are best for your area.

**4**. Rake the soil smooth.

**5**. With the hoe or trowel, dig shallow trenches or holes for the seeds or plants. Plant the seeds of each kind of plant in a row or section by itself. The seed envelope or seedling pack will tell you how far apart and how deep to plant the seeds. Cover the seeds lightly with soil, using the hoe or rake. Tap the soil down gently on top of the seeds.

**6**. If you are planting seedlings, use the trowel to make a small hole in the dirt for each plant, and set the plant in the hole. Fill the hole with soil, and gently press the soil around the plant to hold the plant firmly in place.

**7**. If you wish, write the names of the vegetables you have planted on some flat wooden or plastic sticks with waterproof ink, and stick them in the soil next to the plantings.

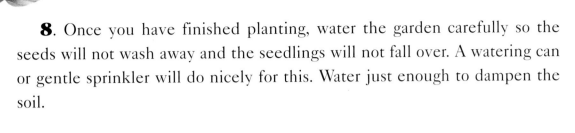

**8**. Once you have finished planting, water the garden carefully so the seeds will not wash away and the seedlings will not fall over. A watering can or gentle sprinkler will do nicely for this. Water just enough to dampen the soil.

**9**. Water your garden often, especially if there is no rain. As the plants get larger and stronger, you will need to water them more thoroughly.

**10**. In a few weeks after planting, you can begin to harvest some of your early crops, such as radishes, lettuce, and spinach. It will not be much longer until the other vegetables are ready.

**11**. If you do not have enough space for a garden in your yard, you can plant vegetables and herbs in a window box or a large flowerpot set in a sunny spot. Tomato plants, for instance, grow very well in pots.

*At the head of the bed she set up the goose-feather pillows,*
*and spread the pillow-shams against them.*
*On each white pillow-sham two little birds*
*were outlined with red thread.*
LITTLE HOUSE ON THE PRAIRIE

# Ma's Embroidered Pillow-Sham

The Ingalls family mostly packed practical items in their covered wagon when they traveled from Wisconsin all the way to Indian Territory. Some of these items also added beauty to their small cabin on the empty prairie—Ma's colorful patchwork quilts and braided rugs, the red-checkered table-cloth, the china shepherdess, and embroidered pillow-shams for the new bedstead Pa had built.

First, Pa made a bedstead of oak slabs that he had smoothed and pegged together himself. "I can't wait to see it made up," said Ma. Then Ma filled the straw tick with clean, dry prairie grass and laid it in the new bedstead. Next, she spread sheets and her prettiest patchwork quilt on top, and placed the feather pillows against the headboard. Finally, she laid the pillow-shams over the pillows.

Ma's pillow-shams were single pieces of white cloth that covered the pillows. At night they were folded up until morning. They made the bed and the one-room cabin look pretty all day.

To make your own red-and-white pillow-sham, you will need:

*Piece of white cotton fabric (26" x 22" for a standard-size pillow)*
*Iron*
*Scissors*
*Needle*

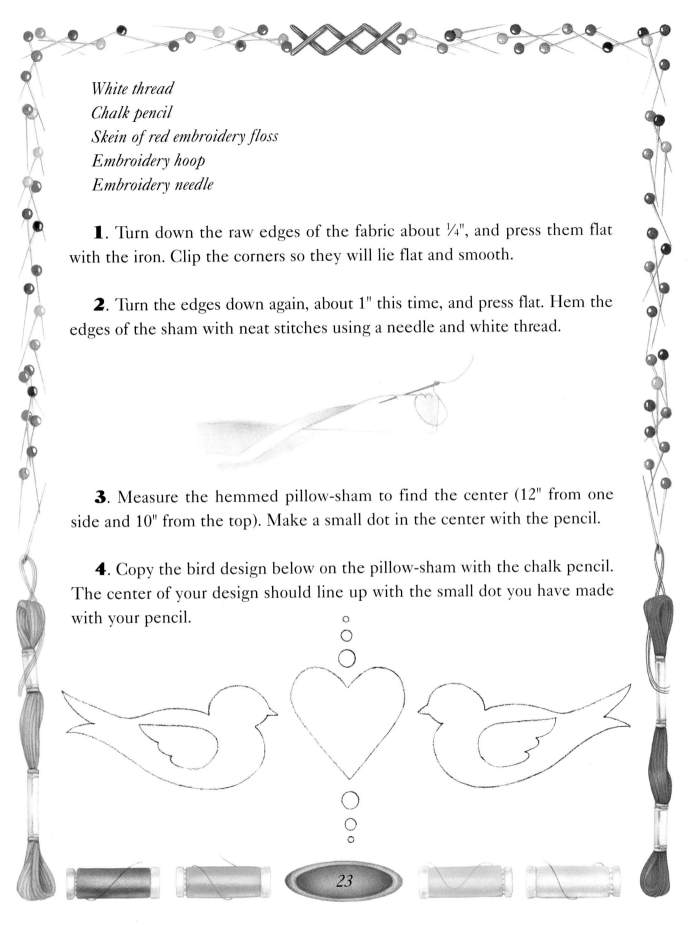

*White thread*
*Chalk pencil*
*Skein of red embroidery floss*
*Embroidery hoop*
*Embroidery needle*

**1**. Turn down the raw edges of the fabric about ¼", and press them flat with the iron. Clip the corners so they will lie flat and smooth.

**2**. Turn the edges down again, about 1" this time, and press flat. Hem the edges of the sham with neat stitches using a needle and white thread.

**3**. Measure the hemmed pillow-sham to find the center (12" from one side and 10" from the top). Make a small dot in the center with the pencil.

**4**. Copy the bird design below on the pillow-sham with the chalk pencil. The center of your design should line up with the small dot you have made with your pencil.

**5**. Once you are satisfied with the way your design looks, place the pillow-sham in the embroidery hoop with as much of the design inside the hoop as possible. This will keep the fabric taut so that stitching will be easier and neater. You can move the hoop to a different area of fabric as needed.

**6**. Cut a 24" length of embroidery floss from the skein. Separate the six threads into three parts, with two threads in each part. Thread the embroidery needle with one of these double threads, tying a small knot at one end.

**7**. Using the chain stitch shown below, embroider the design, following the lines you have drawn. Move the embroidery hoop, and rethread the needle as necessary.

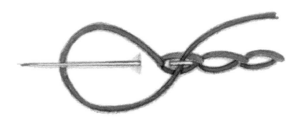

**8**. When you have finished embroidering the design, remove the embroidery hoop. Press the pillow-sham on the wrong side.

**9**. Lay the pillow-sham on top of the pillow on your bed.

*Over the center-table hung an air-castle.*
*Alice had made it of clean yellow wheat-straws,*
*set together airily, with bits of bright-colored cloth at the corners.*
*It swayed and quivered in the slightest breath of air,*
*and the lamplight ran gleaming along the golden straw.*
FARMER BOY

# Alice's Straw Air-Castle

Popular handicrafts of the mid and late 1800s included needlework of all kinds, including crewel embroidery and lace-making. Other crafts were quite elaborate and required more materials. Many women hand-painted china and made decorative arrangements from feathers, wax, beads, and even hair. Air-castles made from the hollow straws of harvested wheat and barley were popular decorations, too, especially in farmhouses like the Wilders'. These air-castles may have been introduced to America by Scandinavian immigrants who settled on farms throughout New York State in the nineteenth century.

To make a straw air-castle, you will need:

*Bundle of dried wheat straws (available at most craft stores)*
*Fine brass or florist wire (22 gauge)*
*Piece of heavy white or clear thread, 24" long*
*7 strips of bright calico, ¼" by 6"*
*Heavy-duty scissors or wire snips*

**1**. Cut the wheat straws into 6-inch lengths, leaving the heads on.

**2**. On a flat surface, lay three straws with heads in a triangle, as shown on the next page.

**3**. Twist a 2" piece of wire around the straw at each intersection to hold the straws together securely, and clip off the ends of the wire.

**4**. Make another straw triangle just like the first one, and set it aside.

**5**. With a piece of wire, attach a length of straw, head down, to each corner of the first triangle. Bring the other ends together at the top to form a pyramid. Wire the tops of the straws together.

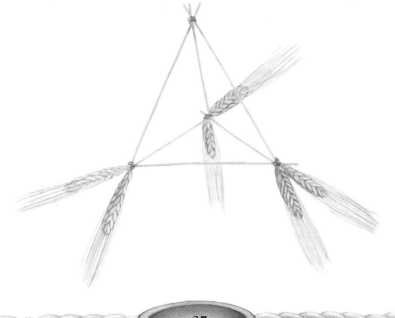

**6**. Make a hanging loop by running a 24" length of thread under the joined straws at the top. Tie the ends of the thread together in a firm knot.

**7**. Wire a few wheat heads to the top point as decoration.

**8**. To make a second tier, run a 10" piece of wire through the center of one of the headless straws, so that there are 2" of wire sticking out of each end. Attach the straw to one corner of the triangle base by twisting one end of the wire around the wheat straws. Repeat with two more straws and two more 10" pieces of wire.

**9**. With the remaining loose ends of the wires, attach the second triangle base (from step 4) to the vertical straws. Snip off any excess wire.

**10**. Tie a strip of colored cloth at each corner. Hang the air-castle on a porch or doorway or ceiling so that it will catch "the slightest breath of air."

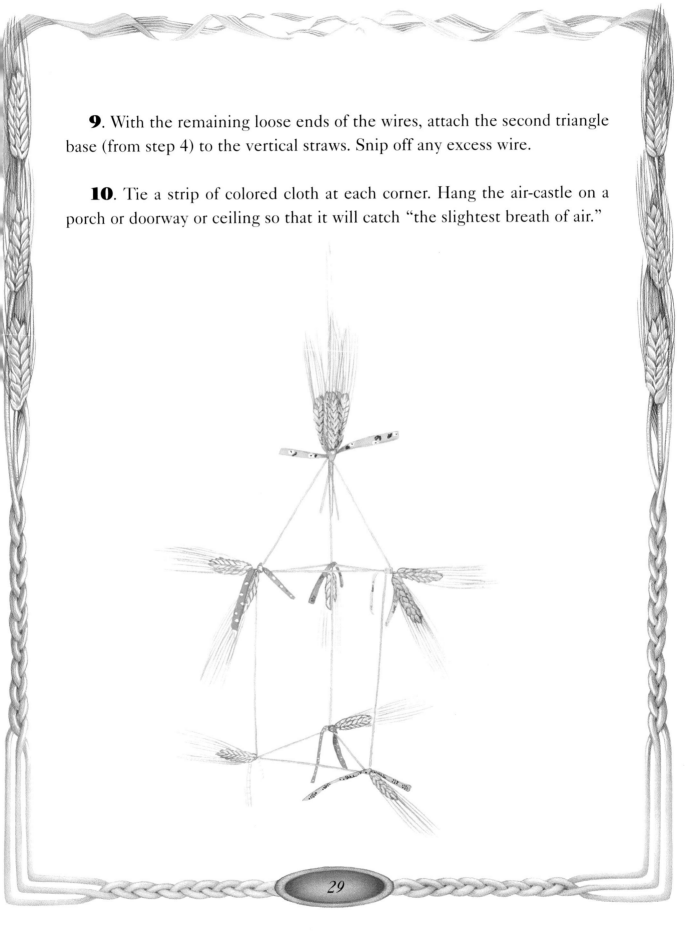

# Baby Carrie's Button String

When Laura was growing up, every home had its button box, because buttons were too precious to throw away. When clothes wore out, the buttons were removed and stored in the button box until they were sewn onto other garments.

In Ma's button box, there were buttons she had saved from her childhood in Wisconsin and even buttons *her* mother had saved from *her* childhood, back in Massachusetts. Some of the buttons came from shops or peddlers, and some were carved by hand.

Mary and Laura could spend hours sitting on their quilt-covered bed in the dugout, running their fingers through the box full of colorful buttons made of glass, wood, bone, shell, silver, and brass. The buttons were in all shapes, too. Some looked like juicy blackberries, and some had tiny raised castles and bridges and trees on them. There was even a tiny button in the shape of a dog's head!

To make a button string, you will need:

*Heavy thread, 10" to 12" long, or longer if you wish*
*Lots of buttons in many colors and shapes*
*Embroidery needle (optional)*
*White glue (optional)*

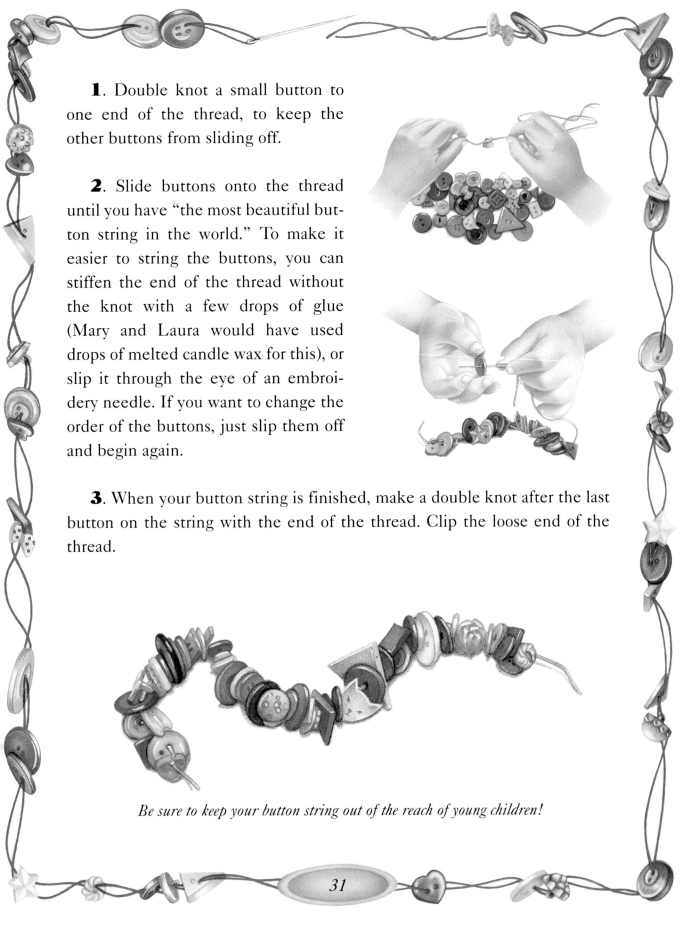

**1**. Double knot a small button to one end of the thread, to keep the other buttons from sliding off.

**2**. Slide buttons onto the thread until you have "the most beautiful button string in the world." To make it easier to string the buttons, you can stiffen the end of the thread without the knot with a few drops of glue (Mary and Laura would have used drops of melted candle wax for this), or slip it through the eye of an embroidery needle. If you want to change the order of the buttons, just slip them off and begin again.

**3**. When your button string is finished, make a double knot after the last button on the string with the end of the thread. Clip the loose end of the thread.

*Be sure to keep your button string out of the reach of young children!*

*Mary was still sewing nine-patch blocks. Now Laura started a bear's-track quilt.*
*It was harder than a nine-patch, because there were bias seams, very hard to make smooth.*
*Every seam must be exactly right before Ma would let her make another, and often*
*Laura worked several days on one short seam.*
ON THE BANKS OF PLUM CREEK

# Laura's Bear's-Track Quilt Pillow

During the long prairie winters, Mary and Laura worked on their patch-work quilt squares. Mary had been sewing her nine-patch squares since she was six years old in the little house in the Big Woods. Laura worked on nine-patch squares, too, in the little house on the prairie. But now she was starting a new pattern, called a bear's track. She was nine years old, and Mary was eleven.

The bear's-track pattern is a variation of a very popular pioneer quilt pattern called a bear's paw. It is made of small triangles and squares in the shape of a bear's paw. The dark triangles make up the bear's sharp claws. In the bear's-track pattern, the colors are reversed, and the light triangles represent the imprint of the bear's claws on the dark path.

To make a bear's-track quilt pillow, you will need:

*Piece of dark cloth, 28½" x 4¼"*       *Ruler*
    *(or enough to make up 112 square inches)*      *Pins*
*Piece of white cloth, 4¼" x 8¼"*      *Needle*
*Piece of coordinating cloth for backing,*      *Thread*
    *11" x 11"*      *Pillow stuffing*
*Scissors*

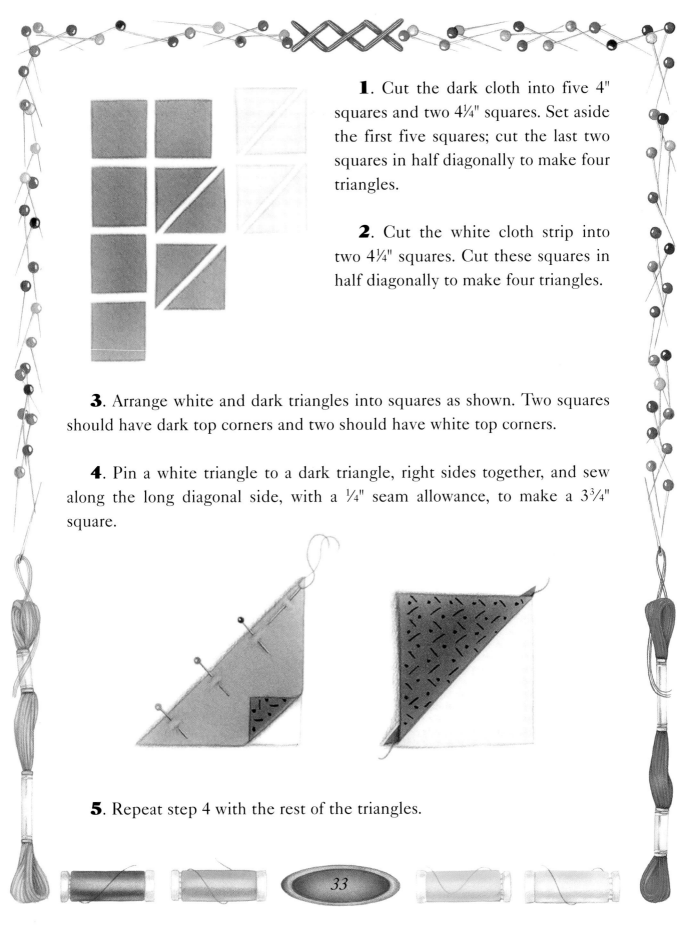

**1**. Cut the dark cloth into five 4" squares and two 4¼" squares. Set aside the first five squares; cut the last two squares in half diagonally to make four triangles.

**2**. Cut the white cloth strip into two 4¼" squares. Cut these squares in half diagonally to make four triangles.

**3**. Arrange white and dark triangles into squares as shown. Two squares should have dark top corners and two should have white top corners.

**4**. Pin a white triangle to a dark triangle, right sides together, and sew along the long diagonal side, with a ¼" seam allowance, to make a 3¾" square.

**5**. Repeat step 4 with the rest of the triangles.

**6**. Pin the two dark-light squares right sides together so that the triangles alternate dark-light-dark-light, as shown below. Stitch the squares together along one side, with a ¼" seam allowance, to make a two-square strip.

**7**. Repeat step 6 with the other two light-dark squares, this time making a light-dark-light-dark strip. Set these strips aside.

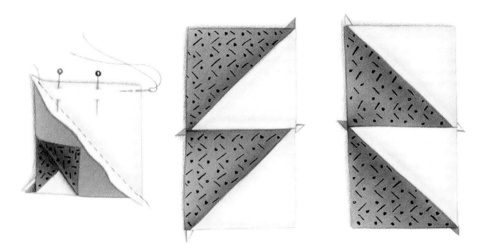

**8**. Sew four dark squares together with a running stitch, ¼" from the edges, as shown, to make one 7½" square.

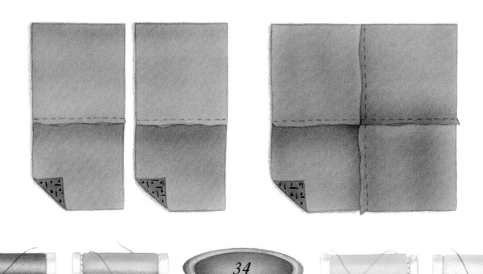

**9**. Pin the remaining dark square from step 1 to the white end of the dark-light strip, right sides together. Stitch the squares along one side so that you have a strip 4" x 11½". This is piece A.

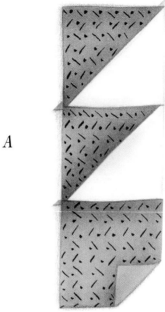

*A*

**10**. Pin and sew the remaining light-dark strip to one side of the large dark square from step 3, so that the white triangles are next to the dark square. This is piece B.

*B*

**11**. Piece A and B together so that the white triangles in A are next to the large dark square in B, and the small dark square in A is at the bottom left corner of the entire block. Sew to make a square.

*A*          *B*

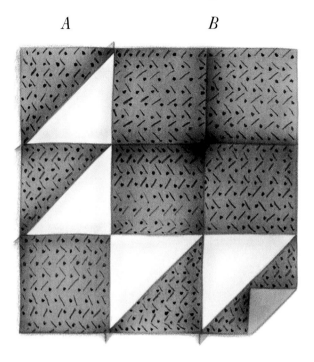

**12**. Press the square so that the seams lie flat and the top is smooth.

**13**. Trim the 11" square of cloth to fit your patchwork square. Pin them with right sides together, and stitch a ¼" seam almost all around the square. Begin sewing in the center of one side, and stop sewing about 3" before you reach the place where you began.

**14**. Clip the corners and turn the square inside out.

**15**. Stuff the square with pillow stuffing.

**16**. Stitch the opening closed with small, neat stitches, and clip the ends of the thread. Your bear's-track pillow is finished. To make a bear's-track quilt for your bed, you would need to sew 24 or more blocks!

# Mary's Christmas Tassels

The bed shoes were Mary's Christmas present from Laura and Carrie when they were living in the Surveyors' House on Silver Lake. They are a good example of how the Ingalls family made use of everything they had, even old and worn material.

Laura and Carrie may have made the tassels for Mary's bed shoes with red or green yarn to match the stripes in the slippers. You can make yours any color you like.

To make tassels to trim a pair of bedroom slippers, you will need:

*Light-weight yarn, any color*
*2" x 2" piece of cardboard*
*Scissors*
*Thread to match the yarn*
*Needle*

**1**. Wind the yarn around the cardboard 12 to 20 times, depending on how thick you want your tassel to be.

**2**. Cut the yarn, and slip the end under the loops on the card.

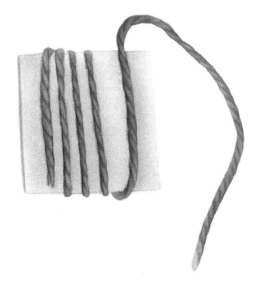

**3**. Cut a 12" piece of yarn, and slip it between the loops and the card. Tie the yarn in a tight knot to pull and hold the loops together.

**4**. Slide the loops off the card.

**5**. Tightly wind another 12" piece of yarn several times around the tassel, about one third of the way down from the top where your first piece of yarn is tied. Tie in a firm knot.

**6**. Cut the loops of yarn at the bottom of the bundle, and trim the ends evenly.

**7**. Shake the yarn to fluff it.

**8**. With matching thread, sew the top of the tassel to your bedroom slipper, or tie it on with the yarn loop at the top of the tassel.

**9**. Make another tassel for your other bedroom slipper and attach it to the slipper. The tassels will bounce on top of the slippers as you walk.

*You can also make tassels to sew to the edges of Laura's Woolen Hood and Muffler (pages 46–49) or to the corners of the Bear's-Track Pillow (pages 32–37).*

*"I hope you and Carrie didn't let the biscuits burn, Mary."*
*"No, Ma," Mary said, and Carrie showed her the biscuits wrapped in a clean cloth to keep warm.*
BY THE SHORES OF SILVER LAKE

# Ma's Cross-Stitched Breadcloth

Breadcloths were necessary items for the table in Laura's day, for not only did they keep the bread warm throughout the meal, but they also kept flies away from the bread. Since breadcloths were on the table at almost every meal, they were often decorated with lace edging or cross-stitched designs to make them attractive.

To make a simple breadcloth with a cross-stitched design that would complement a red-checked tablecloth like Ma's, you will need:

*White linen or cotton fabric, 18" x 18"*
*White thread*
*Needle*
*Pencil (optional)*
*Embroidery hoop*
*Skein of red embroidery floss*
*Scissors*
*Embroidery needle*
*Iron*

**1**. Hem the edges of the linen or cotton fabric using the white thread and sewing needle. If you prefer, you can fringe the edges by pulling out the fabric threads around the edges of the square until the fringe is about ½" deep.

**2**. Sketch the design for the border on one corner of the fabric (as shown below in actual size). The bottom edges of the cross-stitches should be about ½" from the hem or fringe.

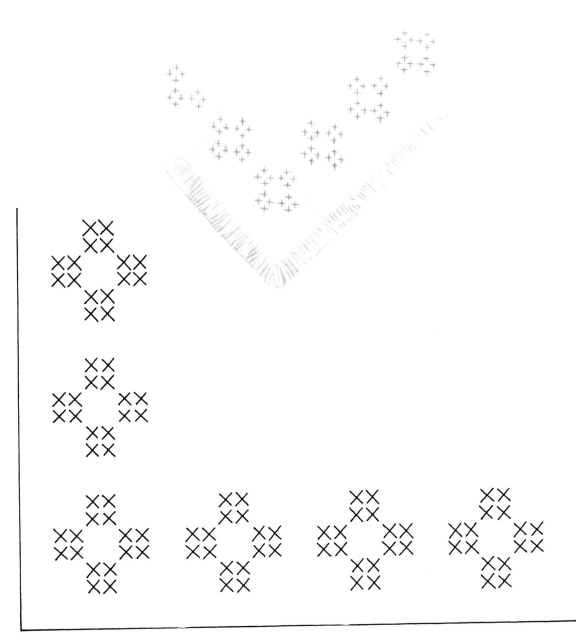

*actual size*

**3**. Place the area of the cloth square that you want to embroider in the embroidery hoop. This will keep the fabric taut so that stitching will be easier and neater. You can move the hoop to a different area of the fabric as needed.

**4**. Cut a 24" length of embroidery floss and use two of the six threads in the floss for embroidering the cross-stitched design. Thread the embroidery needle with the two threads, and tie a knot at one end.

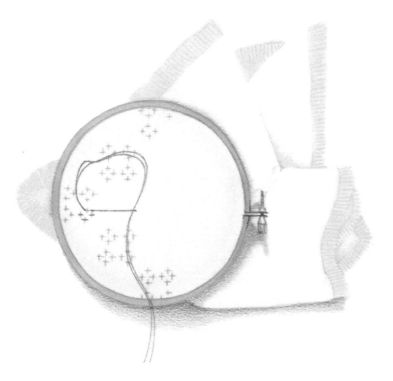

**5**. Starting at the corner, cross-stitch one small block of four crosses, making sure that you keep the top, cross-over stitches going in the same direction, either all going to the right or all going to the left. It is sometimes easier to do all the bottom diagonal stitches in a block first, then go back over them with the top diagonal stitches. You can knot the thread at the end of the block and cut it before you start the next block, or carry the thread over to the next block.

**6**. After you complete the first block of four crosses, move to another block of four in the grouping. Skip two squares to the right of the middle row of squares, and begin cross-stitching the next block. Start with the middle row, and stitch the entire block as you did in step 5.

**7**. Stitch another block to the left side of the first block, so that you now have three blocks decorating the corner. Press flat with a warm iron. If you like, you can cross-stitch the design all around the border of the cloth.

**8**. To use the breadcloth, place warm bread, rolls, or biscuits in the center of the cloth, fold the corners of the cloth diagonally over the bread, ending with the corner with the embroidered design on the top. Place the wrapped bread in a basket or on a bread plate.

*"Here is your breakfast fuel, Caroline," Pa said, laying his armful down by the stove.*
*"Good hard sticks of hay. I guess they will burn all right."*
THE LONG WINTER

# Pa and Laura's Hay Sticks

When the supply of coal ran out in De Smet, there was no other fuel left. So Pa gathered the long grass that grew in the Big Slough about a mile from town and twisted it tightly into small "sticks" to burn in the big black cookstove. These sticks kept the Ingallses from freezing during the long winter.

The hay sticks burned quickly, so Pa spent all day in the lean-to, twisting the hay. Laura wanted to help him. So for months during that long winter, Pa and Laura twisted hay to keep the fire in the stove going.

To make a modern version of Pa and Laura's hay sticks, you will need:

*Hay, or a bundle of natural raffia (available at craft stores)*

**1**. Unfold the raffia so that all the strands are spread out for their full length, about 6 feet.

**2**. Take a "double handful" of hay or raffia from the bundle. Starting at one end, begin twisting the hay or raffia strands tightly together into a rope.

**3**. With your right hand, put the twisted part of the hay or raffia under your left elbow, while your left hand continues to hold the rest of the hay or raffia. Hold the twisted hay or raffia tight to your side with your elbow to keep it from untwisting.

**4**. Take the loose hay or raffia from your left hand into your right hand and slide your left hand backward along the hay or raffia, as close to the twisted rope as possible.

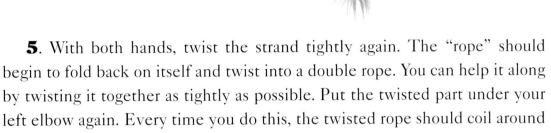

**5**. With both hands, twist the strand tightly again. The "rope" should begin to fold back on itself and twist into a double rope. You can help it along by twisting it together as tightly as possible. Put the twisted part under your left elbow again. Every time you do this, the twisted rope should coil around itself.

**6**. Continue twisting and coiling the whole length of hay or raffia strands until they are "twisted tight and kinking in the middle."

**7**. Tuck the ends of the hay or raffia into the last kink of the twisted rope. Bend the twist a bit if necessary, so that you can slip the ends in between the kinks, and let it twist itself back tight, as Pa and Laura did.

Put several of these hay sticks in a basket on the hearth.

*Laura put on Pa's old coat and her hood and muffler*
*and went into the lean-to with Pa.*
THE LONG WINTER

# Laura's Woolen Hood and Muffler

Laura had to wrap herself in her warmest clothes to sit in the lean-to while she and Pa twisted hay for fuel. The lean-to was a little room built onto the kitchen of Pa's building in town. It was not heated and was made of only one layer of boards, so while it was a shelter from the fierce prairie winds, it was bitterly cold. Laura wore her hood and muffler over her coat to keep her head and neck warm.

In *Little Town on the Prairie*, Laura again wears her hood and muffler to go to her first "sociable," a small party at Mrs. Tinkham's:

*Laura put on her brown coat and set carefully over her head her peaked hood of brown woolen lined with blue. The brown and the blue edges of cloth were pinked, and the hood had long ends that wound around her neck like a muffler.*

To make a hood and muffler, you will need:

*Brown wool fabric, 12" x 52"*
*Light-blue wool fabric, 12" x 52"*
*Pins*
*Brown thread*
*Needle*
*Scissors*
*Pinking shears*

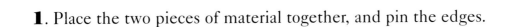

**1**. Place the two pieces of material together, and pin the edges.

**2**. Using a simple running stitch, sew by hand or machine all around the edges, leaving a ½" seam allowance.

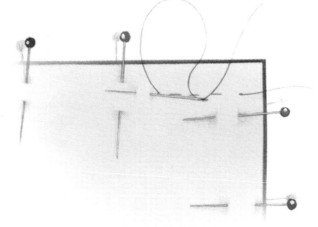

**3**. Trim the edges with pinking shears. This will make a pretty zigzag edge all around and also will keep the wool from unraveling.

**4**. Fold the muffler in half with the blue lining on the inside to make four layers. The folded muffler should measure 12" x 26".

12"

26"

**5**. To form the hood, place a pin to use as a marker 9" down from the fold on one side. Pin all four layers of wool together in a few places, from the top fold to the marker pin.

**6**. Stitch the layers together along the back seam line, starting at the top fold and ending 9" down at the marker pin. Make two or three extra stitches at the end for added strength. This closes up the back of the muffler and forms the hood.

**7**. To wear the hood and muffler, place the hood on your head, fold the front edge back about two inches so that the blue lining shows around your face. Now cross the long ends of the muffler across your throat and place them over your shoulders.

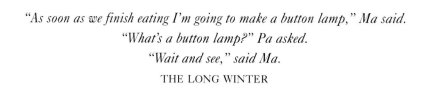

*"As soon as we finish eating I'm going to make a button lamp," Ma said.*
*"What's a button lamp?" Pa asked.*
*"Wait and see," said Ma.*
THE LONG WINTER

# Ma's Button Lamp

During the long winter, the kerosene for the lamps ran out. But Ma remembered the button lamps from her childhood in eastern Wisconsin "before this newfangled kerosene was ever heard of." All she needed was some grease. Pa found a box of axle grease, and Ma showed the girls how to make a button lamp.

First, she spread some of the axle grease on an old saucer. She made a wick from one of Pa's overcoat buttons and a square of calico. She greased the calico wick and set it in the saucer. When she lit the tip of the wick, "a tiny flame flickered and grew stronger. It burned steadily, melting the axle grease and drawing it up through the cloth into itself, keeping itself alight by burning. The little flame was like the flame of a candle in the dark."

To make a decorative button lamp, you will need:

*6" square piece of calico*                                      *Scissors*
*Large flat button, about 1" in diameter*      *Small basket (optional)*
*Piece of thread, 18" long (any color or colors)*

**1**. Spread the square of calico right side down on a flat surface.

**2**. Set the button in the center of the square. Bring the corners of the square together, and bunch the calico tightly around the button.

**3**. Tightly wrap the piece of thread several times around the twisted calico as close to the button as you can. Leave about 6" of thread on each end.

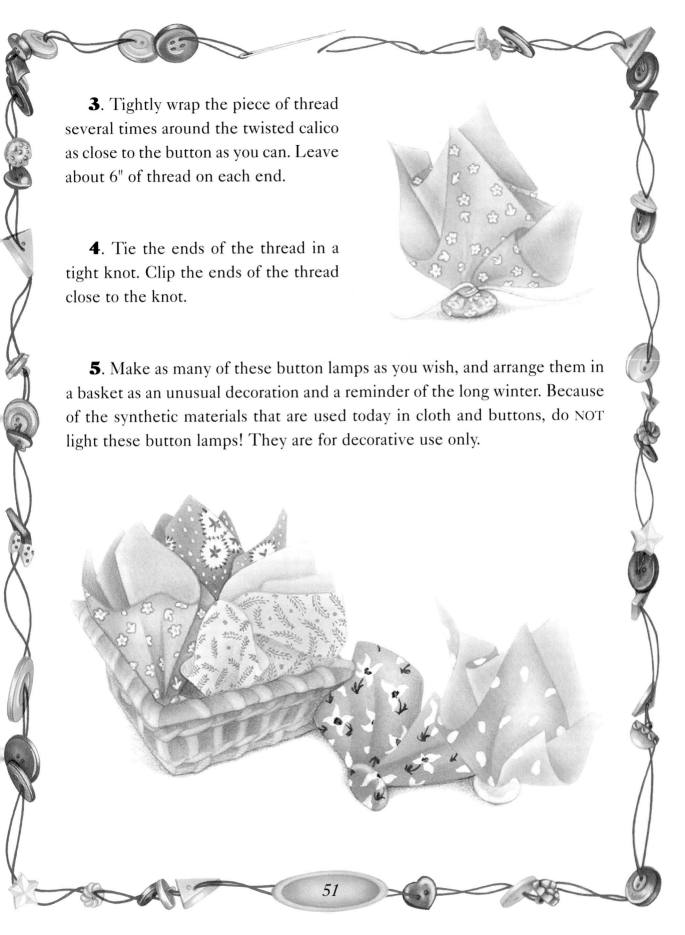

**4**. Tie the ends of the thread in a tight knot. Clip the ends of the thread close to the knot.

**5**. Make as many of these button lamps as you wish, and arrange them in a basket as an unusual decoration and a reminder of the long winter. Because of the synthetic materials that are used today in cloth and buttons, do NOT light these button lamps! They are for decorative use only.

# Little Town Party Napkins

Ben Woodworth invited several school friends to his house for a birthday supper. Laura had never been in such a beautiful house. The Woodworths even had a separate room "only for eating in." The table was beautifully set with china and silver and fancifully folded napkins.

In Laura's day, the only napkins available were cloth napkins, generally made of cotton or linen. Today many people use paper napkins, especially for everyday family meals. To make folded napkins, though, cloth napkins work best, and they make any occasion extra special.

To make a flower-folded napkin you will need:

*A large cloth napkin, at least 16" square, for each place at the table*

**1**. If possible, lightly starch the napkin; it will be much easier to fold and will hold its shape better.

**2**. Spread the napkin flat on a surface, right side down, with one corner at the top, so that the napkin looks like a diamond.

**3**. Fold the bottom half up so that you now have a triangle. Crease the bottom edge.

**4**. Bring the two side corners up to the top point so that you have a diamond shape again. Crease the side edges.

**5**. Fold the bottom corner up about three fourths of the way to the top corner. Crease the bottom edge.

**6**. Fold the two side corners around to the back, and tuck one corner into the other to hold it.

**7**. Gently pull down the front point.

**8**. Now pull down the next two points at the top so that they flare out at the sides. Leave the last double point standing up straight.

**9**. Fold a napkin for each place at the table. You can set the flower-folded napkins to the left of the dinner plates and forks if there is a first course already on the plates, as there was at the Woodworths'; or, if the plates are empty before the guests sit down, you can set the napkins in the center of the plates.

*Most marvelous of all, in front of each plate was an orange. Not only that; for those oranges, too, had been made into flowers. The orange's peel had been cut down from the top in little pointed sections, and each section was curled inward and down, like a flower's red-gold petals. Held within these petals, the flesh of the orange curved up, covered with its thin, white skin.*

LITTLE TOWN ON THE PRAIRIE

# Little Town Orange Flowers

At Ben Woodworth's party there was a delicious supper of oyster soup, potato patties, codfish balls, and biscuits. Then there was a birthday cake and beautiful orange "flowers" for dessert. The oranges at Ben Woodworth's birthday party were a rare treat for Laura. She was fourteen years old and had tasted an orange only once before, in Walnut Grove. She was not even sure how to eat a whole one!

To make an orange flower, you will need:

*One orange per person (oranges with thin rinds work best)*
*A small sharp knife and a blunt knife, or an orange-peeler*

**1**. Wash the oranges, and let them dry completely.

**2**. With the tip of the sharp knife or the cutting point of the orange-peeler, carefully cut just through the orange peel from the top to about ½" from the bottom of the orange. Do not cut into the fruit!

**3**. Repeat all around the orange, making narrow strips.

**4**. With a blunt knife or the curved end of the orange-peeler, carefully loosen each strip of peel from the fruit. Make sure you don't break off the strips.

**5**. Gently spread the strips away from the fruit. Roll the tip of each strip inward, down toward the bottom of the orange, and wedge it slightly between the fruit and attached part of the peel. If the orange peel is too thick to roll easily, you can scrape off some of the inside white part with a grapefruit spoon or knife.

**6**. Set the orange on a plate, and serve.

*For Ma there was a lamp mat of woven braid, with a fringe all around it of many-colored beads strung on stout thread.*
THESE HAPPY GOLDEN YEARS

# Mary's Beaded Lamp Mat

After being away at school for two years, Mary finally came home for a few weeks. She brought gifts that she had made herself—a blue-and-white beaded bracelet for Laura, a pink-and-white beaded ring for Carrie, and a little red-and-green beaded chair for Grace, the youngest in the family. And for Ma she had made a braided mat with a bead fringe, to set under the kerosene lamp.

To make a braided mat, you will need:

*5 yards narrow woven braid or cord (available at fabric stores)*
*Scissors*
*Thread*
*Needle*
*3 to 4 ounces small beads in assorted colors*

**1**. Wind the braid around in a spiral, stitching it on the underside as you go.

**2**. When you are about an inch from the end, cut the end of the braid diagonally.

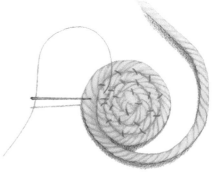

**3**. Turn the raw edge under slightly and stitch it securely to the bottom of the mat.

**4**. Thread the needle with a length of thread. Bring both ends of the thread and tie them together in a knot.

**5**. Tie a bead securely onto the end of the double thread. Slip enough beads over the needle and onto the thread, letting them slide all the way to the end.

**6**. Stitch the fringe to the edge of the mat with several stitches. The top bead should just touch the edge of the mat. Make a knot on the underside of the mat and clip the thread.

**7**. Repeat steps 5 and 6 until you have fringes all the way around the mat. The fringes should be spaced a half inch apart, and they should be about ½" to 1" long.

*You can set the mat under a lamp, as Ma did. You can also use it under a hot dish or plant, or even use it as a doll's rug.*

Laura's gift was a bracelet of blue and white beads strung on thread and woven together, and Carrie's was a ring of pink and white beads interwoven.

THESE HAPPY GOLDEN YEARS

# Mary's Beaded Bracelet and Ring

When Mary gave Laura the bracelet she had made, Laura wondered how Mary could keep all the different-colored beads in order. "Some seeing person puts the different colors in separate boxes," Mary explained. "Then we only have to remember where they are."

To make a beaded bracelet or ring, you will need:

*At least two colors of small beads*
*Heavy-duty thread*
*Needle*
*Bracelet fastener (available at craft stores)*

**1**. Measure your wrist or finger. Cut three pieces of thread, each about 12" longer than the measurement.

**2**. Thread a needle with one piece of thread, and tie a bead onto the thread about 5" from the end.

**3**. Slip beads one at a time over the needle.

**4**. String enough beads on the thread to go around your wrist or finger, plus about ½" extra.

**5**. Tie the last bead onto the thread. There should be about 5" of thread left on either end of the beaded string.

**6**. Carefully remove the needle. Set the string aside.

**7**. Make two more strings of beads the same way. Fasten the three strings together at one end by tying the ends to each other.

**8**. Loosely braid the beaded strings, and check to see if the bracelet or ring will fit. (If necessary, braid the strings more tightly, or add or remove some beads, to make it fit.)

**9**. Tie the remaining thread ends together.

**10**. If you are making a bracelet, tie one half of the bracelet fastener on each end of the combined beaded strings, right next to the beads. Clip off the extra thread.

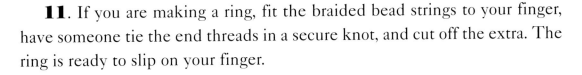

**11**. If you are making a ring, fit the braided bead strings to your finger, have someone tie the end threads in a secure knot, and cut off the extra. The ring is ready to slip on your finger.

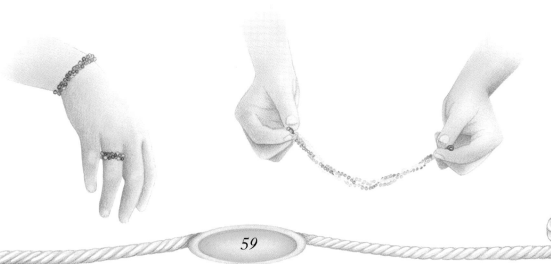

# Laura's Golden Wheat-Sheaf Bread

Becoming an expert at breadmaking like Laura takes a lot of practice. Laura had seen Ma make the salt-rising bread in the little house in the Big Woods, and the prairie cornbread that, according to Pa, needed only Ma's handprint on top for sweetening. "Light bread" was yet another kind of bread; it was made of yeast and white flour, both small luxuries on the prairie.

While we do not have Laura's own recipe for light bread, the following recipe, adapted from a cookbook published in the 1800s, is typical of the old-fashioned light breads from Laura's day. You can make a plain, everyday loaf or a decorative loaf with the same wheat-sheaf design that adorned Laura and Almanzo's glass bread plate.

To make a loaf of Golden Wheat-Sheaf Bread, you will need:

*2 cups milk*
*2 tablespoons sugar*
*1½ teaspoons salt*
*1 tablespoon shortening*
*Food thermometer (optional)*
*¼ ounce (1 envelope) active dry yeast*
*¼ cup warm water (110–115 degrees)*

*6 cups all-purpose unbleached flour*
*1 beaten egg*
*Food thermometer (optional)*

**1.** Heat the milk in a saucepan, stirring occasionally, until the milk is almost to the boiling point. When a few bubbles start to form around the edges and steam begins to rise from the milk, it should be ready.

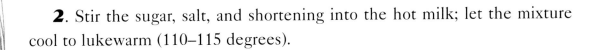

**2**. Stir the sugar, salt, and shortening into the hot milk; let the mixture cool to lukewarm (110–115 degrees).

**3**. Meanwhile, stir the yeast into the warm water until it is dissolved. Set the mixture aside to "proof." If the yeast is good, the mixture will thicken and be bubbly after about 5 minutes. If it does not, try again, using new yeast.

**4**. In a large bowl, combine the proven yeast and 3 cups of the flour with the lukewarm milk mixture. Beat the mixture with a wooden spoon until the batter is smooth.

**5**. Add the remaining flour, one cup at a time, mixing well after each addition.

**6**. Turn the dough out onto a lightly floured board, and cover it with a clean damp cloth. Let the dough rest for 10 minutes.

**7**. With floured hands, knead the dough for 8 to 10 minutes. To knead dough, push the palms of both your hands into the dough, spreading the dough out slightly. Fold the dough back over itself, and turn it slightly clockwise. Repeat the pushing, folding, and turning for 8 to 10 minutes, or until the dough becomes very smooth and elastic. Sprinkle more flour on the board and your hands if the dough gets sticky.

**8**. Form the dough into a ball, and place it in a lightly greased bowl. Turn the dough over in the bowl so that it is greased all over.

**9**. Cover the bowl with a cloth, and set it in a warm place so the dough can rise until doubled in size (approximately 1 to 1½ hours). To make sure the bread has risen enough, poke two fingers straight down into the dough about an inch. If the dents stay, the dough has risen enough. If they fill up quickly, let the dough rise awhile longer.

**10**. Punch the risen dough down with your fist, turn it over in the bowl, cover it with a clean cloth, and let it rise again until it is double in size, about 45 minutes.

**11**. Turn the dough onto a greased baking sheet. Set aside about a cupful of the dough. Form the remaining dough into an oval loaf about 15" long and about 8" wide at the top and about 5" wide at the bottom.

**12**. To make the wheat-sheaf shape, cut strips of dough about a ½" wide and about 9" long, starting at the top of the loaf. Spread the strips of dough out slightly to form the top part of the wheat sheaf. Trim the top edges as needed.

**13**. Cut or score deeply the bottom few inches of the loaf to resemble the bottom stalks of the wheat sheaf. The cuts should be ½" wide and about 4" long. You do not have to spread these strips apart as you did in step 12.

**14**. Divide the set-aside dough into 3 equal parts. Roll each part into an 8" long strip. Braid the strips together.

**15**. Lay the braid across the center of the wheat-sheaf loaf. Tuck the ends under the loaf.

**16**. Cover the loaf with a clean damp cloth, and set it in a warm place to rise until it is double in size, about an hour.

**17**. Brush the beaten egg lightly over the top and sides of the loaf. Bake the loaf in a preheated 400 degree oven for 35 minutes, or until it is golden brown. When it is done, the loaf will sound hollow when you tap it on the bottom.

**18**. Remove the loaf from the baking sheet, and set it on a wire rack to cool.

**19**. You can wrap the Golden Wheat-Sheaf Bread in Ma's Cross-Stitched Breadcloth, if you like.

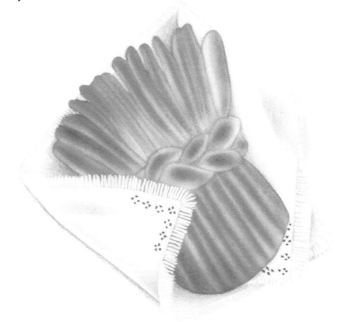

# Index